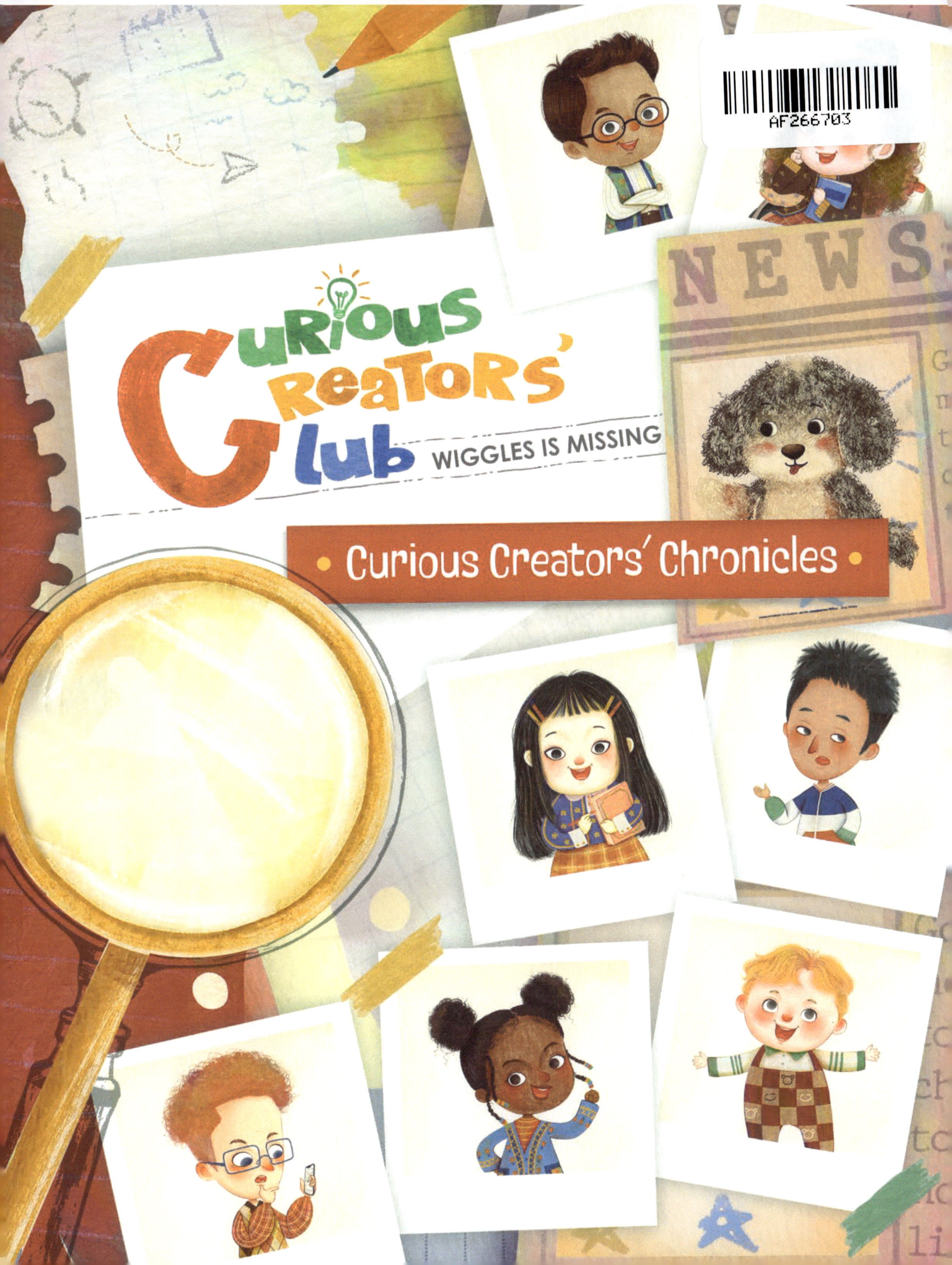

CURIOUS CREATORS' Club
WIGGLES IS MISSING
NEWS
Curious Creators' Chronicles

ISBN: 978-1-967024-16-2
First printed edition, 2026

EDLINKS® Press LLC
PO Box 205
Essex Junction, VT 05453
USA
www.edlinkspress.com
edlinkspress@edlinks.com

For information about purchases, special requests, and educational needs,
contact EDLINKS® Press at edlinkspress@edlinks.com or visit
Curiosity2Create at www.curiosity2create.org

CLUBHOUSE GUIDLINES
1. Everyone has the right to be heard.
2. Be kind (to each other, to materials, etc).
3. Ask questions with an open mind.
4. Be kind to yourself.
5. Don't give up— try, then try again.
6. Be supportive of your fellow mystery solvers.
7. Have fun.

Follow along with the instructions for each week's activity!
Write in it!
Doodle in it!
How to use your Chronicles
Be Creative in it!
Be fearless in it!
Take Risks In It!
(look for borders & doodles to get creative with!)

Curious Creators Contract

This is your official recruit contract! This contract is between you, your teacher, and your teammates, and it lays out the guidelines for how Investigators can be the best they can be. Read through the contract carefully, and when you're ready, go ahead and sign your name at the bottom.

CONTRACT

I am unique

I will be a good team player

I will actively listen to those around me

I will be respectful to other

I will ask questions

I will come up with many ideas

I will use my creativity and curiosity to solve problems

I will be open-minded

I will have fun!

____

____

____

___________________________   ___________________

Signature   Date

TEAM NAME BRAINSTORM

In the boxes below, write or draw some team name ideas below. You do not have to fill them all!

THE 5 W'S!
{MY IDEAS!}

In the boxes below, write or draw what you think the 5 W's stand for!

W
W
W
W
W

THE 5 W'S!

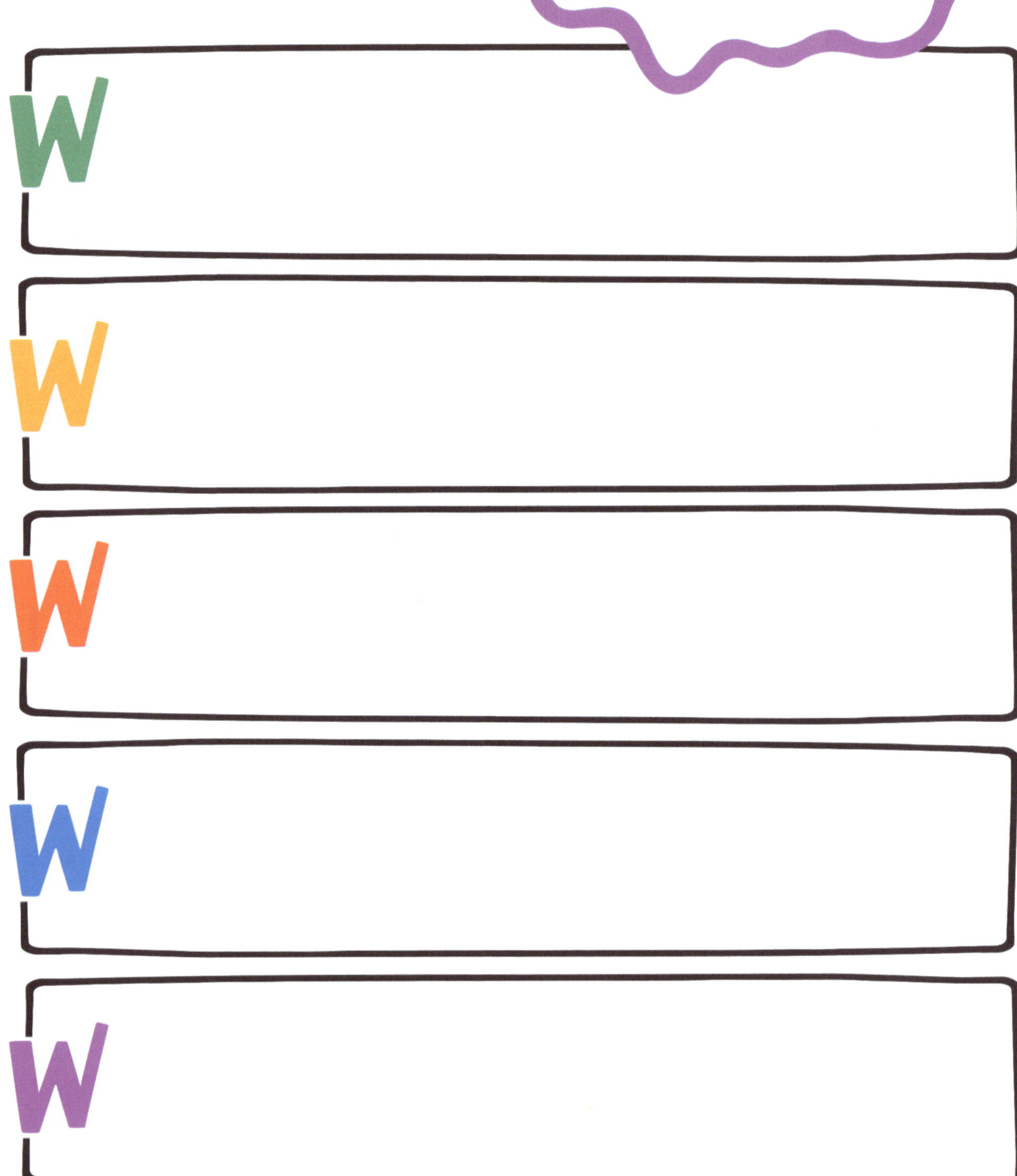

The 5 W's help us ask key questions when trying to find solutions to a problem.

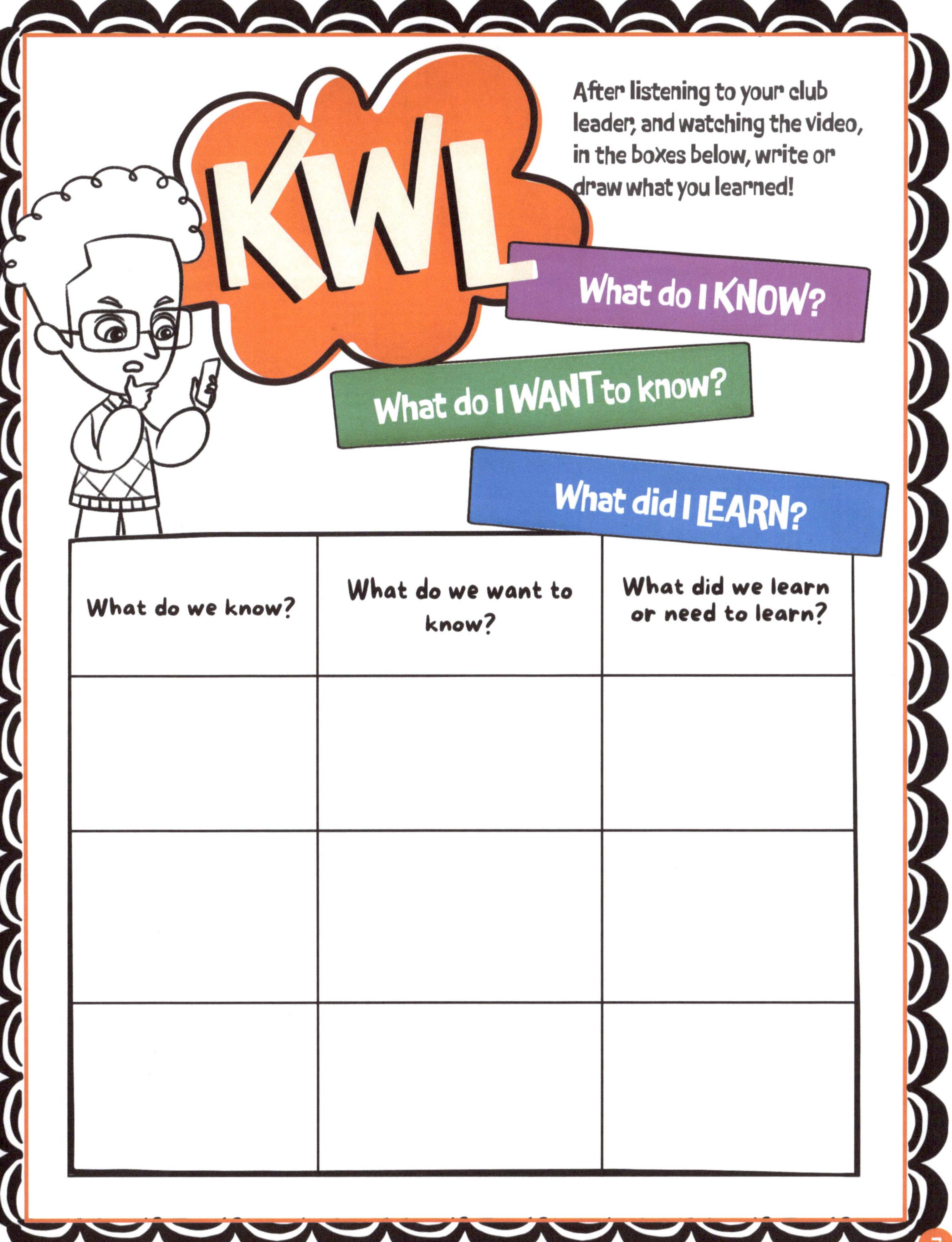

KWL
After listening to your club leader, and watching the video, in the boxes below, write or draw what you learned!
What do I KNOW?
What do I WANT to know?
What did I LEARN?
What do we know?
What do we want to know?
What did we learn or need to learn?

Tips and tricks for finding clues!
1 Listen to the information carefully
2 Reread or rewatch
3 Use our senses to gather information
4 Pick out key terms or facts
5 Answer the 5 W's

Write Down Your Clues!

In the boxes below, write or draw clues that you hear in each video.

Abby Video

Playground Video

Veterinary Video

Town Center Video

EXAMPLE OF MISSING DOG POSTER

MISSING DOG!

WIGGLES

Breed: Mixed Breed
Color: White, Brown, Black
Emotions: Friendly & Playful

Wiggles has been missing since this morning. He was last seen in Charlie's backyard. Charlie accidentally left the back door open!

REWARD: CERTIFICATE

CALL OR TEXT IF FOUND
CHARLIE'S MOM: 555-123-4567

ROUGH DRAFT OF YOUR MISSING DOG POSTER

Invention Directions

1 With your Group Think of Ideas for your invention.

2 Choose which one you want to make.

3 Use the materials your club House leader provides to make a prototype.

4 Your invention does not have to activly work, it can simply represent what you would build.

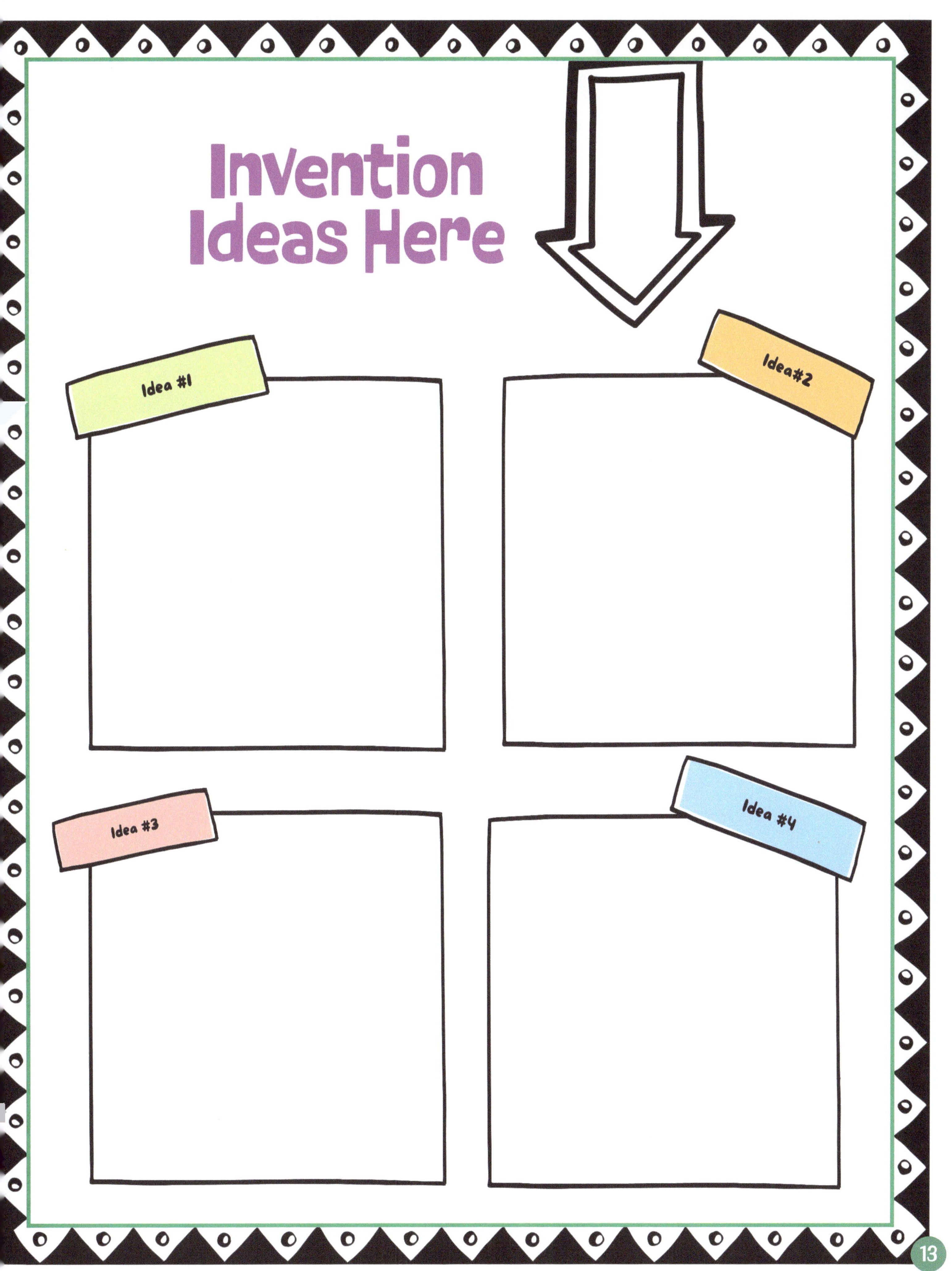

Invention Ideas Here
Idea #1
Idea#2
Idea #3
Idea #4

Invention
Design Here

One Time I Failed...

...But That's Okay!

Write or Draw one time you failed that you're willing to shrae with the club! Remember...we are going to celebrate our failures!

Invention Feeback!

In the boxes below, write or draw, 1-2 things you liked about each team's invention!

Team #1

Team #2

Team #3

Team #4

Team #5
Team #6
Your Team

CREATIVITY NAVIGATOR
ACTIVE LISTENER
CURIOSITY CHAMPION
18

RISK-TAKER
CURIOUS CREATOR
PARTNERSHIP PRO

9 781967 024162